3-DAY SELF-DEFENCE MANUAL

by
BRONILYN SMITH
4th degree blackbelt AIKIDO

First published in 1987 by
Lilyfield Publishers Pty Ltd
2 Aquatic Drive Frenchs Forest NSW 2086 Australia
Publisher: Nicholas Brash

National Library of Australia
Cataloguing-in-Publication data

Smith, Bronilyn.
The three-day self-defence manual.

Includes index,
ISBN 0 7301 0209 2.

1. Self-defence for women – Handbooks, manuals, etc. I. Title.

613.6'6'088042

Designed by Warren Penney
Typeset in Sydney
Printed by Globe Press, Melbourne

Foreword

After many years as a self-defence instructor, consultant and lecturer it has become apparent there is a need for a book which provides simple, straightforward self-defence advice, where physical strength and skills are not essential. In dealing with and teaching people from very wide-ranging backgrounds and abilities, it is obvious that people are looking for personal protection skills they feel *they can cope with.* What has been missing, or misinterpreted from self-defence information in the past, has been basic common sense. So much of what we need to know to protect ourselves and our families is in fact just that, *common sense*, but it is only of value when it is recognised as such.

How often have we looked at the simplicity of an expert demonstrating anything, and thought 'how easy that looks' and 'it's just common sense', or 'why didn't I think of that?'. Again it's not until we are presented with what appears to be an obvious solution, that we recognise those simple elements for ourselves!

This book is designed so that basic information is easily recognised and remembered. It is self-defence for the uninitiated, from the young to the elderly, and for all lifestyles.

While facts and figures are essential in establishing needs such as where a problem exists and how far it extends, they are kept to a minimum here as people have indicated they like an 'information book' to quickly and clearly tell them what *they want to know*.

This is a good news book. We all have our own personal difficulties, and we have problems within our communities but *The Three-Day Self-Defence Manual* is meant to emphasise positive solutions rather than dwell on our fears. *This is your guide for staying out of trouble.*

Many horrifying statistics on the incidence of rape and violence can be quoted but, like all statistics, they mean little unless you *personally* are part of those statistics. Don't let this happen.

Preplanning may help prevent you becoming 'another statistic'. Think through some of the things which you feel may be potentially dangerous or threatening, then given the background information you have on personal safety, decide what you would do in such circumstances. The key to self-defence is awareness. Your ignorance is an attacker's advantage. *Don't allow them* the advantage of surprise.

We need a *change of attitude*, not only from others but from within ourselves. *The Three-Day Self-Defence Manual* aims to inform – make people think for themselves, and realise the positive steps they can take.

Contents

Introduction

So what *is* self-defence? It is in fact a means by which we can protect ourselves from those who would do us harm. At its most simplistic self-defence can mean avoiding, where possible, the need to use a physical technique. Self-defence *is* for everybody.

To learn a martial art can be very rewarding at a personal development level and can be an excellent form of self-defence, but for most people the training and discipline required to participate fully is just not within their scope. However people who have little physical skill can easily absorb and use the defences described in this book. The handy hints are reinforced with cartoon drawings which enable a situation to be quickly grasped and appreciated. 'First-hand situations' are also used to consolidate this information.

Too often in the past self-defence has been considered a rather questionable need, reserved perhaps for the more unconventional and/or those 'looking for trouble'. But today almost everyone from teenagers to grannies, from office executives to retired couples, has recognised the need for at least a basic knowledge of simple self-protection measures.

HOW TO USE YOUR THREE-DAY SELF-DEFENCE MANUAL

Follow these easy steps and you will find that you can defend yourself. You do not necessarily have to be fit, clever or strong.

DAY 1

Step 1 The first thing you need to recognise, or learn is that we all have the right to protect ourselves. Refer to *pages 7 & 14*.

With some planning, particularly looking at preventive measures, you need not feel helpless and defenceless. Nor should you have to set unrealistic limitations on the way you dress, where you work, how and when you travel.

Step 2 When under threat you must respond positively, and not be half-hearted – use your total energy to effect. Refer to *page 17*.

Step 3 Read any sections of the book which appeal or are particularly relevant such as those on self-defence for the elderly, when travelling, for parents and so on. Then look at some of the things in particular which make our homes safer. Refer to *pages 52-56*, also Handy Hints on *pages 57-62, 95 & 96*.

Step 4 To see how this information can help you read 'Situations' on *pages 32, 59-62, 86 & 96*.

Step 5 Now some physical tips.

Recognise your own 'weapons' and how to use them. Try some of these simple tips. Use your head, your hands, elbows and thumbs. Refer to *pages 34, 39-41*.

Be aware of the power of a swinging arm, effective fists, including the V fist, and so on. Refer to *pages 39-41*.

These are easy to learn, but will feel more 'comfortable' when practised. Try each technique at least ten times.

Read 'Situations' on *pages 47 & 50*. What do you think your could do?

Step 6 Finish Day 1 with more practical tips such as what to do if you receive an obscene phone call. Refer to *pages 74 & 76*.

DAY 2

Look at what you need to know when out, on foot or in the car; simple measures to take when travelling.

Step 1 Read 'Self-Defence When Walking', *pages 64-70*; 'Car Safety', *pages 71-73*; 'Weapons', *pages 30-37* and some of the Handy Hints on *pages 27-29, 66 & 72*.

Step 2 Be aware of some of the things you can do when travelling. Refer to *pages 21-29*.

Step 3 Add to your own 'weapons'. Refer to *pages 43-44 & 46*.

Also look at some of the things which can be used to help protect us and those items we are likely to carry with us. Refer to *pages 17, 47-48 & 66*.

Step 4 Practise using some of those 'weapons' we carry with us such as keys, magazines and so on. Refer to *pages 28, & 48-50.*

Step 5 Read Handy Hints on *pages 18-20, 43, 46 & 70.*

There's some more physical practice here, particularly with a co-operative partner. Try the exercises out – you will find they work well.

Step 6 Read 'Situations' on *pages 32, 44, 49-50, 62 & 68.*

DAY 2 practice has added to the simple techniques and responses learned on Day 1, and Day 3 rounds off your self-defence knowledge.

DAY 3

Whether you practised the physical tips, or sat and read, by now you know the basic essentials; how to make yourself, your home and going out a great deal safer. You are less likely to be the victim. With the simple physical skills, this knowledge is extended even further.

HERE ARE SOME SIMPLE CHECK LISTS

When attacked

- Use what you have: hands, elbows, fingers, fingernails, feet, knees, head and voice.
- Use what you may carry with you (or have within reach): keys, magazines, comb, brush, handbag, shopping bags, baskets, umbrella, walking stick, torch, a biro, book or bedlamp.

These are all things you can use to strike or thrust at an attacker.

When alone

- Pretend there is someone else in the house.
- Check *before* opening the door.
- Always ask for identification.
- Know your own home layout and what you can do in an emergency, where you can go for help. Pre-arrange a distress signal with a neighbour.

When out

- Be alert, walk purposefully, be aware of what you are carrying.
- Don't put your purse on top of a basket, etc.
- If asked a question keep some distance. Walk on the lighted side of a street and avoid doorways, etc.
- Carry a torch for light, or as a weapon.
- Have keys in your hand to jab at an attacker.
- You can carry a personal alarm, but be prepared to use your voice. You can also carry a whistle.
- Park in well-lit areas and keep doors locked.

Home safety

- Take basic safety precautions such as securing windows and not leaving keys in locks.
- Front and back doors should be of solid construction and preferably with strong security doors fitted.
- Use safety chains, or door limiters and peepholes to check before letting someone in.
- There are many security aids from electronic systems to battery-operated alarms.
- The location of phones in the home is important.
- There are also wireless intercoms, personal

alarms and other products for safety in the home which can be considered.

• Read 'Situations' on *pages 44, 49 & 50*, and recap the physical techniques practised on Days 1 and 2. See how easy they now feel.

CONGRATULATIONS! You have completed your basic Three-Day Self-Defence Plan.

The Three-Day Plan provides simple, easy to remember hints and techniques. Always keep your Manual handy for quick reference.

Let's Put Self-Defence In Perspective

Too often our first reaction to the words 'self-defence' is negative. Why? It's not because we don't want to protect ourselves. What then? Self-defence situations are usually shown as ugly and frightening, and this is not the way ordinary people want to see themselves involved. Added to this is the television image of self-defence which leaps to mind for most people. While this image usually performs with dramatic and devastating effect, it does not necessarily fit within what we see as our own generally more limited physical capabilities.

Everyone has the right to personal protection, and a knowledge of self-defence gives the ability to exercise that right. This means we need to know how to protect not only ourselves, but also our families – especially our children, our teenagers and our older people. It is a community effort.

Self-defence is a survival skill, it is as necessary as a basic knowledge of first aid or water safety. We all hope we don't have to use those skills, but most would prefer to know 'something' in case of emergency. After all, it may save a life or prevent an injury. So too can
self-defence!

Self-Defence Is A Plus Factor

'Quality of life', 'self-esteem' and 'self-image' have all become frequently used catchwords. An essential element in one's ability to experience all these things is a belief in one's own capabilities. Physical and mental well-being go hand in hand. If we have a low estimation of our physical ability, at any level, then mental well-being and confidence are also affected. Recent scientific studies reinforce the view that no matter how small the physical achievement, there is a measured increase in mental well-being.

Increasingly we find ourselves living in a community which demands self-sufficiency and self-reliance, from our young people through to our senior citizens. What can we do to meet this increasing demand for self-sufficiency?

We must take the time to examine our own needs, consider what we want to do, where we live, where we want to go. Some people have become deeply introverted, afraid to go out, yet afraid to be at home because fear for their personal safety has become so intense. This is not for us, so think ahead, preplan what you actually *could do* in an emergency. Preventive self-defence is the best form of self-defence.

With a positive attitude to your personal safety

when you are away or at home – perhaps alone – you can relax a little within yourself and enjoy being yourself, you are not totally helpless and defenceless.

Self-defence is a very definite *plus factor.*

Overcoming The Fear Factor

Too often we set limitations on ourselves, and our children, simply because we are afraid to discuss our fears – often choosing to blame something else. Think about it – how often have we told our children they must not be out after dark, or restricted ourselves to being home 'by dusk'?

Of course this can be a sensible precaution, but it is not the darkness we should be afraid of. Let's get that quite clear. It's what can happen so much more easily, given the cover of darkness. We must talk about these dangers rather than use darkness as the fear factor.

Whilst darkness can aid a potential attacker, it can work equally *in your favour* – help you to get away! The attacker cannot easily see any counter-move you make, and it's easier for you to slip out of sight using the darkness.

Certainly *be prepared* for possible dangers which may lurk in the dark, but remember there are advantages – use them.

SUPERMARKET

Self-Defence – When To Use It

Avoid potentially dangerous situations where possible. If there is an opportunity to safely run from a dangerous situation, *then run*! However, if you are unable to escape and you know you are going to be hurt if you don't fight, *then fight.*

Don't be half-hearted about it. You must use your total energy and use it effectively.
Don't run at half-pace.
When running, kick high-heeled shoes off if necessary.
Your shoe can even be used as a weapon – high-heeled shoes particularly can be a very useful weapon on your feet or in your hands!

The things you might normally be carrying – an umbrella, 'hefty' handbag or schoolbag, a hockey stick, even a walking stick, or perhaps grocery bags – can all be used by you. They can be dropped on feet for example, *thrown or hit at* your attacker. All can be most effective 'distraction' tools in protecting yourself, but you must think ahead, recognise their potential usefulness and be prepared to use them. Remember an injured attacker cannot move as quickly and he will also be more identifiable
to police.

HANDY HINT

When grabbed by the hair press your hands down tightly over the attacker's hand. This stops the immediate pain and allows you time for counter-measures – kicking, screaming, etc.

While holding his hand tightly against your head, jerk your head down sharply. This puts sudden and painful pressure on the attacker's wrist. This applies whether grabbed by the hair in front, the side, or behind.

HANDY HINT

When pinching take a *small* piece of flesh as this is more effective. Inner thighs are highly sensitive. If both arms are trapped behind, in a bear hug for example, then to gain a momentary loosening of the grip you are in an ideal position to make use of this vulnerability.

Alternatively, if the situation is one requiring more drastic measures, then you are in a good position to strike a strong blow backwards using a hand blade or fist into the groin, or squeeze and twist the testicles. But if this is necessary, remember there can be no half-measures – under such circumstances you cannot afford to *half* injure someone, the attacker must be totally incapacitated!

The same technique can be applied if you are lying down, particularly if someone is sitting astride. By pinching, particularly the inner thigh region you can cause the attacker to momentarily 'lift up'. In that instant he is more easily rolled off to the side. Again if more drastic measures are needed there can be no half-measures here either, but if you strike accurately and hard there is no doubt he will be doubled up, writhing in pain.

HANDY HINT

When you are being held, regardless of whether it is from in front or behind, always be prepared to *twist or turn* vigorously *sideways.* Pulling backwards or forwards against the grip wastes energy, and is far less effective. You will find it becomes extremely difficult to maintain a hold when the grip is *twisted against.*

Think how difficult it is to hold a squirming object – from children to animals or fish!

Public Transport And Self-Defence When Travelling

Using public transport is in many cases a necessity, and should be something we can all do without undue concern for our personal safety. Unfortunately this is not the case in many cities which are plagued with assault and intimidation on buses and trains to the point of real stress and worry for commuters and travellers alike. This is not restricted to larger cities, country areas also experience problems where isolation and long distances can give rise to difficulties, too. But public transport should be a facility that can be enjoyed free of such problems. A time to catch up on some reading, a chat with a friend or just plain dozing to pass the time away. So what can we do to help make ourselves less vulnerable and better equipped to sidestep dangers, whether real or potential?

First, always check timetables. Knowing your times helps avoid long waits in what can frequently be lonely and exposed locations. Given this type of situation you may find yourself an easy target for unwanted attention. This attention can vary from verbal harassment and offers (of many kinds!) to possible abduction.

Always carry the necessary coins for an emergency phone call. For example, if you have missed your bus or train then you can let someone know where you are and make alternative arrangements. Most forms of public transport have phone facilities at the station, or nearby, so whenever possible make yourself familiar with their location, then you know where to go quickly if the necessity arises.

If a railway platform or bus depot is virtually deserted, wait near the entrance, don't wander away to more isolated places. At night stand in the lighted ticket office area, or in other areas where people are more likely to be found. If waiting at a bus stop or taxi rank, wherever possible stand near a lighted area such as a shop window or house.

When travelling another hazard, which afflicts females in particular, is the 'groper', or the wandering hands. For women commuting on trains, buses and trams, particularly in peak hour, this unwanted attention happens all too frequently. You can deal with it in a number of ways, from a simple vocal response to a physical action. Your response may well depend on circumstances at the time and the reaction it will in turn cause. Vocally the direct 'get your hand off my leg!'delivered in a loud voice, or a more subtle response can be very successful. If you have a few stock phrases ready you won't find yourself panicked or embarrassed into silent endurance. Physical responses can also vary. You may simply slide your hand over his until you have a finger (little finger preferably), then

FARES

bend it back *sharply.* Little fingers are very vulnerable. It is unlikely he will try that move again in a hurry!

Crowded bus stops or packed stations are a pickpocket's paradise so make this paradise a little harder to achieve by taking a few simple precautions. Be alert – if you feel yourself pushed from behind, bumped in a crowded street or if someone stops suddenly in front of you, you may well have just been 'rolled'. If this happens react *immediately* and look directly at the person you suspect as you check your wallet or purse. Your bag should always be kept firmly shut, and held securely, particularly in crowded conditions. It is important to consider how you carry a handbag and what type you use. Some are definitely easier targets for a thief. Purses should not be left on top of shopping bags or supermarket trolleys. Nor should they be left on the floor, or next to your seat in a cafeteria, restaurant and so on. Also be wary of hanging handbags on the back of toilet doors, there has been many an instance of bags disappearing 'over the top'. *The best type of bag is one which appears difficult to steal.*

Travelling overseas the loss of a wallet or purse can be even more important as it may well be not only your money which is lost, but airline tickets, passport, driver's licence and credit cards. These items can be a great deal harder to replace quickly and certainly cause more inconvenience. There are many safer ways of carrying your money and a travel goods store, for example, can show you a

number of innovative products made for carrying money and papers more securely. These can include lightweight document/money pouches which are mainly carried inside clothing and around, say, the waist.

When travelling on trains, particularly at night, take notice of your fellow passengers' movements so you don't suddenly find yourself isolated with a potential attacker. If you find this has happened be prepared to get out at the next station and change carriages to one with more people. Try and sit near a conductor, or in an aisle seat, but if this is not possible sit next to an emergency handle, or communication cord, and be prepared to use them – but only in a real emergency.

Reports suggest theft from travellers both local and overseas has increased. We tend to be careless, providing an easy target – how often have we seen suitcases, for example, left unattended near the hotel entrance while our traveller registers at the desk or pays the taxi?

When travelling check your room thoroughly on arrival, ensuring that windows are properly secured. Keep the chain or door limiter 'on' once you have entered your room. This should apply particularly when watching TV or in the bathroom and so on. When staying in a high risk area you may choose to leave the radio or TV on when you go out and put the 'do not disturb' sign on the door so your room is less likely to be entered. On returning to your room have the keys in your hand, and if you feel you are being followed along the passage, return to the reception desk if necessary. Rather than get in the lift with another person late at night don't be afraid to use your intuition, wait for another lift, or ask for a member of the hotel staff to see you to your room if you feel that is warranted.

The main factors in protecting yourself, whatever the circumstances are to think ahead – whether commuting to and from work, school, or travelling longer distances and perhaps in unfamiliar territory. Take stock of what you've got and think positively about what you can do, then you may even relax a little yet not present an easy target. As most attackers are opportunists use the common sense precautions described and don't give them that chance.

HANDY HINT

There are personal battery-operated alarms which can be hand held and can be used inside or outside the home. Hung on a bedroom or hotel room door the alarm can provide extra security as when activated it emits a loud piercing sound. With the necessary attachment plugged in, the alarm is set off if the door is opened. As with all battery-operated products there can be malfunctions so always look at what *you can do* for yourself, with the alarms as a very useful extra.

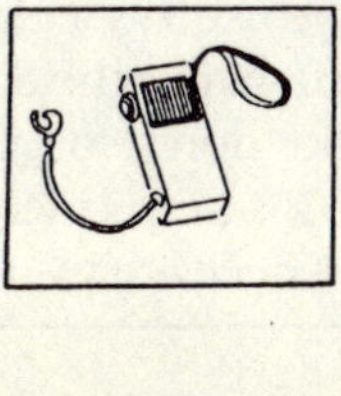

HANDY HINT

Rather than carry a specific weapon be aware of what is to hand and improvise when necessary.

A rolled up newspaper or magazine can be an effective self-defence tool. A magazine, any size, can be quickly rolled to form a pointed end. By grasping the magazine tightly approximately 7-10 cm from the point you can strike a very powerful blow.

The magazine can be effectively driven into, or hit at almost any part of the body, for example the attacker's temples, eyes, windpipe, forehead, stomach, kidneys or groin. To yell loudly or scream 'KIAI' can give added power and confidence.

Have a practice. Obviously, as with any self-defence move, confidence in your own ability is important. Practice in quickly rolling and striking with a magazine will bring this confidence. A newspaper or magazine is something you are likely to have when you are travelling or waiting at a station. It is also a good idea to keep one within easy reach for example in each room of your home, the front seat of the car and so on.

HANDY HINT

Phone box hints – if trapped or someone tries to enter the booth while you are there, look at what you have with you that could be used as a temporary weapon. You can also 'prop' against the door to prevent it being opened and don't forget the obvious, be prepared to ring for help (including no coin emergency numbers if necessary).

KER ST.

POLICE!

Weapons – If Used Against You

If threatened with a deadly weapon a decision has to be made whether to submit, be it temporarily, or fight. Only you can make that decision given the circumstances at the time.

If you can control a very natural reaction to panic, then you have a better chance to assess your opportunities clearly, and perhaps make use of whatever is at hand to help in your defence. Sometimes it may be possible, and preferable, to 'play along with' the attacker until there is an opportunity for you to make a countermove and escape. People have managed to successfully talk their way out of trouble, so if you can maintain your wits and talk then do so. Unfortunately this opportunity is not often there and you need to think through what you could do in such drastic circumstances, then at least you have a *plan of action*. Lack of knowledge, or forethought of your possible options, gives you little or no choice over the action taken.

In a sexual assault, particularly if rape is the motive, there will come a moment when the knife, gun or any weapon must be put down in order to successfully complete the sexual act. That moment could well be the moment you react. If possible fling the weapon out of immediate reach. If an attacker is kneeling on, or next to you, his balance is easily broken when he is *pushed* hard to the side he is kneeling. You can push using your arms if they are free, or bring your legs up and use them to push him sideways. At the same time hit out at your attacker with whatever you can get your hands on – using the element of surprise, and the momentum from a swinging blow. There should be no half-measures – push, shove and hit with *all the energy you have* and get quickly to your feet.

HANDY HINT

A desperate situation can call for desperate measures. The sound of glass shattering can attract attention and cause an attacker to retreat. So be prepared to break a window by throwing something at it if necessary.

If attacked in a public place *any* commotion that brings people to your aid can help so don't let yourself be surprised or embarrassed into silence.

Situation It is the middle of the day and you have an appointment in a city office block. As you hurry into the lift thinking of your meeting, you only vaguely take notice of the man who enters with you. As the lift ascends he pulls out a knife and orders you to press the stop button.

Defence Obviously to struggle with an armed attacker in a confined space would be extremely dangerous. When rape is the intent there will come a moment when the attacker must put down his weapon. Seize that moment and act decisively and strike hard. Hit the lift alarm button and quickly move it onto the next floor to summon help.

In the past police have advised that rapes mostly occurred on Friday and Saturday between 11 p.m. and 3 a.m., but now they occur at all times. So don't be complacent.

HANDY HINT

When entering blocks of units or flats, lifts, etc., be aware of your surroundings, take notice of who enters with you. Have your keys, a magazine or similar in your hand and you will not be easily caught unawares, but remember that not everyone is a potential attacker.

HANDY HINT

You can use your head – literally.

It can for instance be smashed back into the attacker's face (if the attack is from the rear), causing severe pain. 'Using your head' can also work well when both arms are trapped.

OR

use your forehead (if a frontal assault) to crack downwards onto his nose – this should inflict sufficient pain to make him release his grasp. This applies equally well when lying down and you have no other recourse.

Situation You have had a busy morning and have finally put the baby down to sleep, suddenly you hear the back door open and you find yourself being menaced by a man with a knife. What should you do?

Defence The natural inclination would be to panic, but you realise that it is not just you at risk, your baby is also in the house. If you have thought ahead (refer home safety) then for someone to easily enter through an unlocked door would be most unlikely. But, given your present circumstances be alert. This is your kitchen, you know what's in it, *use what you've got.* Most household items can become temporary weapons to be thrown, hit or squirted at an assailant. People have used such things as fly spray, hair spray, room deodorant and so on, which if squirted at an attacker can be a temporary eye irritant, giving you the chance to get help.

Weapons – The Use Of

The carrying of weapons is not recommended for a number of reasons.

1. The weapon may be turned against you unless you are particularly skilled in its use.
2. Under the various States' firearms and dangerous weapons Acts, unless you're licensed to carry a firearm or dangerous weapon you're committing an offence just by carrying one, even if you don't use it.
3. Weapons are difficult to carry and conceal so they are not always at hand when you need them. This also applies to some of the self-defence 'aids' which are promoted from pepper, mace . . . to anti-rape stench capsules, and these may not function correctly at the crucial moment.

Therefore any objects can be used to aid in your defence, but don't be totally dependent on them.

A question often asked is whether people resisting an attacker would get into more trouble than if they were passive. The Director of the United States National Centre for Prevention and Control of Rape has clearly stated that women should *not* be passive. Two surveys sponsored by the Centre of rape victims and victims of attempted rape showed that women who used physical or psychological resistance – who screamed, bit, hit, scratched and kicked and tried to escape – were

more successful in avoiding rape and physical injury generally.

Sixty per cent of the women studied had escaped rape, most of them by fighting back. Both studies showed the more passive the victim the greater the risk of serious injury.

So consider what 'assets' you do have:

- your voice
- hands/knees
- fingers/fingernails
- feet
- elbows
- your head.

Unlike other weapons they are always with you!

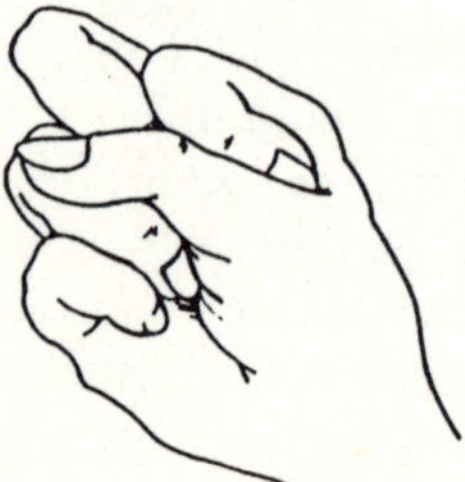

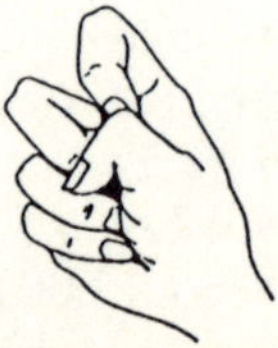

Hands/Elbows

Consider the 'weapons' we always have with us and some of the things we can do without the need for specialist training, martial art expertise, or particular strength and stamina. For example, if attacked from the rear, a well-delivered blow with the *elbow* can be most effective. Take one hand, palm up, in the other and turning sideways, deliver a blow with the full force of your *whole body* behind it – not just your elbow. Driving your elbow back into the solar plexus region or upwards toward the neck/face, depending on the size of the attacker, can be devastating.

Your *thumbs* can be used to jab or press into the area just below the ear lobes. Straight in and up is very painful!

Unless trained in the martial arts, most women have a relatively ineffective punch as their hand is generally small. However a powerful blow can in fact be delivered using the *full momentum of your swinging arm*, particularly if aiming for the sensitive end of the nose. You can strike using your hand open, or closed in a fist. You don't need a hefty hand to cause considerable pain, and it can be delivered as a forward blow, or equally as well backhand – easy to remember, requiring little skill or practice on your part.

One method of forming a more effective *fist*, where size is not important, is to block your thumb tightly against the fingers. At the same time *extend the middle finger knuckle*. This gives a more effective and painful striking force, particularly when aimed at the softer and more vulnerable areas of the face, throat and body.

Alternatively you can also use the V fist. With your palm facing towards you, tuck the top of your first and second fingers tightly back against the base of the fingers to form a V shape, and keep your thumb well tucked in. When you turn your hand over to strike, the V shape is more obvious, and again provides you with a very effective striking blow.

However like many of the new things we learn it may feel a little awkward at first, but as you practise it will feel more comfortable and its potential striking power can be seen – or felt!

The heel of the hand thrust up under the nose or under the chin certainly inflicts a painful blow. Thrusting up and pushing back at the same time works well against not only a standing attack but also if you are lying or have been knocked down.

While specialised training is not required for the techniques described, as with anything involving physical movement a little practice with a co-operative partner can help make clearer in your own mind the particular sequences you will need to put your knowledge to its most effective use. Practice of this kind can even be fun, and need not be overly strenuous unless you wish otherwise. No particular facilities are required and you can have a practice anytime, anywhere, in the home or at work . . . it's up to you.

HANDY HINTS

Little fingers are weakest and therefore the most vulnerable finger so make use of this. Little fingers, the attacker's, can be bent back *sharply*.

The Y shape – with fingers held straight and tightly together one side, and your thumb held straight in the opposite direction, you will see your hand forms a Y shape. Thrust up under the attacker's nose using the base of the Y as the striking point, this too will inflict considerable pain.

If you can scratch, then do so. This is not only painful but can make the attacker more easily recognisable for police identification.

Feet/Knees

Some more of the 'weapons' that are always with us are our feet and knees. The trick is to realise their many 'advantages' and learn how to successfully and *effectively* use them when attacked.

With your feet you can *stamp down hard* on toes or foot, particularly if you are wearing shoes with a heel or solid sole. You can *kick back* into the offender's leg or use your heel to *rake down* his leg from just below the knee to the ankle. This causes intense pain and as with the other moves described should allow you the opportunity to break away.

A knee in the groin is considered by some to be the 'only self-defence women need' – were it only that simple! Although most women and girls are informed of this self-defence, the incidence of its effective use is not as common as we would like. Certainly if you are in a situation where this defence can be used then do so, but well aware of their vulnerability in this area most men position themselves where effective use can be difficult. However if you are in position then always kick or knee to the groin with full force and momentum.

Other vulnerable areas can be kicked, such as just below the knee from in front, or the joint of the knee from behind or the side. Balance is then easily broken forward or backward. You can accelerate the attacker's fall by grabbing the hair, or clothing round the upper shoulders and yanking down hard.

HANDY HINT

If choked from behind by an *arm around the neck*, turn your head towards the crook of his elbow – this will give you an extra breathing pocket. You can now respond positively – really kick back hard or grind your heel down his leg.

Situation You are walking to your car after work, suddenly you feel uneasy, as if there is someone behind you. Before you can turn you feel fingers wrap around your throat from behind, dragging you backwards. What do you do?
Defence First reaction – *chin down* so you can breathe. Next, in order to release his fingers from your throat, slide your hands along to his fingers (*little fingers* preferably), and yank them back *as hard as you can.* The pain will force him to loosen his grip giving you the opportunity to scream, deliver a good kick to the leg, or run – preferably all three!

Your Voice

Consider the possibilities. One American study showed that 60 per cent of all assaults on women which were successfully repelled, were repelled all, or in part, by a loud, clear, sharp *yell*! So whether you are young or old, big or small, learn to use this potentially powerful defence weapon to maximum effect. Many think they know how to yell but sometimes it can come out as no more than a squeak from the throat. Make it a loud '*HIIAAAA*!!' into his face – as you really push your breath out from the stomach region.

You can't successfully yell holding your breath in, so relax as you let it go with all you've got! Have a practice (when no-one's about if you like), you may surprise yourself . . . or the neighbours. You could take the opportunity to practice, and release some of the day's tensions, while driving the car. But windows wound up would be advisable!

A sudden yell or series of screams into the attacker's face will cause him to pull back – at least momentarily. This is your opportunity to quickly get away, or counter the initial grab.

HANDY HINT

Attacked in your home, or in the street, yell '*FIRE*' with all your might – sadly a 'help, help' can draw little or no response. People tend to react more readily to the 'perceived' danger of fire as it may affect them directly or their property.

Situation You have just finished shift work – it is dark as you make your way to the car. Walking alongside the building you are suddenly grabbed and pushed roughly back against the wall, his hands around your throat. Feeling totally helpless – your voice and windpipe cut – what *can* you do?

Defence This is a very common form of attack. However, if you are grabbed by the throat, one of your most powerful defences is your ability to scream or call for help. Rather than futilely pulling back against the grip, your first reaction should be chin down, as close to your neck as possible. This makes it difficult for the attacker to cut off your windpipe or voice box, giving you that all important chance to help yourself. At the very least scream. You can also look at your other weapons:

- feet – stamp, kick and so on
- fingers – scratch, pinch, gouge
- elbows
- your head can be used for butting.

These are just a few. Little skill is needed but you *must not be tentative* in what you do and expect success. If you run, don't run at half-pace – run flat out!

HANDY HINT

There are noise-producing anti-mugging/rape alarms which are generally available from electronic and other specialist stores where this type of product is sold.

Keys

Learning how to make use of the everyday things we have about us should be an essential part of personal protection plans. There are the 'weapons' which are *part of us* such as feet, hands, elbows, voice, etc., and there are the everyday items we are most likely to *carry with us.* Consider such items in this light and you may be surprised how practical they can be in any self-defence strategy.

Keys for example can be used in many ways. They can be a very effective self-defence 'tool', and having them in your hand should become a habit. No more fussing and fidgeting trying to find your keys at the car or house door. They should be *in your hand* ready for a smooth entry or exit – leav-

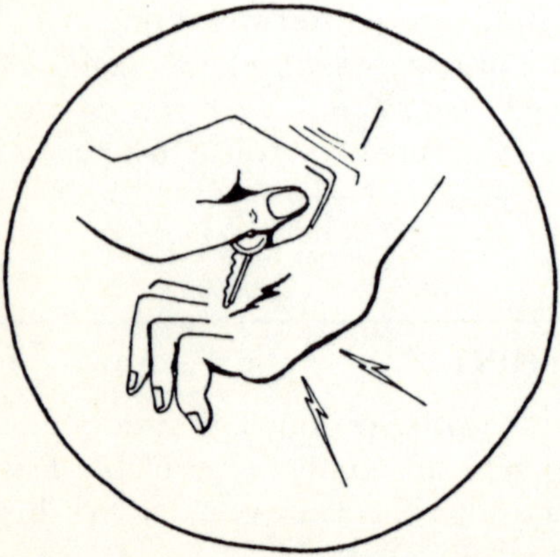

ing very little opportunity for any would-be attacker.

They can also be used as a sharp and effective weapon by positioning one or more keys so they protrude from between the fingers. Be prepared to strike or jab with them, this should prove a nasty surprise for any would-be assailant.

Small and difficult to detect the key can be used as a quick distraction or, if the attack warrants more drastic measures, then it can be used to strike at more vital areas of the body. For example temples or near the eyes, throat (windpipe), side of the neck, groin, ribcage, lower back and up into the armpit – any of these regions can cause extreme pain and injury, so the use of such measures is not to be taken lightly.

HANDY HINTS

As a quick effective move, to jab down onto the back of the hand with your key or into the upper arm (biceps) can be sufficiently painful to effect a release from most grips.

Another simple move is with your hand on top of his pushing down, jab the key *up* into the palm of his hand.

If molested or approached while in the car be prepared to pull keys from the ignition and jab into the attacker to make him draw back.

Situation Although the car park was packed when you arrived it is now almost empty. Walking up to your car you reach into your handbag for the keys.

An assailant suddenly emerges from the shadows taking you completely by surprise as he grabs. Petrified, what could you have done to help prevent the situation?

Defence Be aware of your surroundings *don't* walk blindly into a car park at night, *look around*. Be aware of potential 'lurking' spots and avoid them. Equally important have your keys *in your hand* as you enter the car park. Two purposes, one it will enable you to slip into your car quickly and smoothly, minimising the opportunity for a surprise attack. Secondly, keys thrust into the attacker's face or jabbed into his hand or body can be an effective weapon – giving you the opportunity to get away, fast!

Situation As you enter your block of units the corridor appears deserted. You move quickly towards the lift. Without warning you find yourself grabbed from behind and dragged back into a doorway. What can you do?

Defence For this particular attack (bear hug from behind) a quick but effective move to break the grip is to take his fingers (little finger preferably) and *yank* them back *as hard as you can*!

You can also

- kick
- thrust your head back into his face
- scream
- use your keys to jab at him (get into the habit of having them in your hand – not in your bag!).

You are most definitely not helpless, but don't be half-hearted in your response.

Home Safety

Protection for yourself in your own home, as well as your property, is an important element in home safety. One Australian survey showed that only 68 per cent of breaking and entering crimes were reported to police. High levels of break and enter crimes have continued throughout Australia and while in the majority of instances burglary is the prime motivation, whether intended initially or not, assault and/or rape can ensue.

One police report showed that 38 per cent of homes burgled were entered through an unlocked door or window and a further 27 per cent were burgled after a window had been forced. So let's not make it easy for you to be the victim. Another increasing trend has been for break-ins to take place during daylight hours (about 79 per cent), as this is a time when homes are often unattended.

The important point to realise is that with a break-in/burglary whether there is a physical loss of possessions or not, it is the mental effect which can be just as far reaching and devastating as any loss of property. It can deeply affect people's sense of security and well-being. So what can we do about it?

Why not give yourself a home safety check list and consider some of the following hints very carefully.

Everyone, particularly those living alone should

ensure every window and door is locked before they retire for the night, and that includes upstairs windows.

Similarly make sure windows are covered before undressing – don't give peeping toms a chance.

Locking the doors when vacuuming, in the shower, or even sitting watching television should become a habit as it is all too easy for an intruder to enter without your knowledge. So again learn to minimise potential dangers. When answering the door, particularly if you are alone, take the precaution of intimating that there is someone else in the house, preferably a male. For example you could call out 'I'll get it, Doug!' before you open the door, and ask to see identification before letting a stranger into your home. If in doubt, check. When the caller is genuine this will cause no problem. If you expect the visit of a tradesman or workman and you feel insecure then simply invite a friend over for company.

With more daylight break-ins when the home occupants are generally at work or school, the best protection is efficient visible security, this applies especially to the back of the house. Police advise that the harder you make it for someone to gain entry, the longer it will take. This puts the intruder at risk so they are more likely to move on to an easier target than stay and be caught in the act.

To make your home more secure, external doors should preferably be of solid wood construction and where possible a strong security door fitted to the back as well as front door gives maximum protection so that an unwanted caller has no opportunity to catch you off guard. If you do not have a security door then a peephole and security chain or door limiter can be another alternative. The peephole and security viewer is a simple cylinder fitted with a glass lens. When installed at eye level this allows a viewing angle of approximately 160 degrees so you can easily see who is at your door *before* opening it.

You can protect windows with good quality locks, visible from the outside. Remember flyscreens on windows are no real deterrent to someone entering your home as they can be easily cut.

Few intruders like smashing glass, preferring to force doors or insecure windows, and they usually attack the back of the house first. Don't forget windows on upper floors as intruders can certainly climb, too! Too many rapists and intruders have entered through unlocked or easily entered windows such as the louvre type which can be easily removed. Police advice in such cases has been to ensure windows are secured, so look closely at your own situation. You can obtain key-operated window locks for extra security. These lock securely when the window is closed, or left partly open for ventilation and can be keyed for one-key operation of all secured windows.

While it may be impossible to make a house completely safe, most break-ins are committed by amateurs who spot an easy chance and take advantage of it. You can make the intruder feel uneasy by installing time switches to operate lights, television, radio, etc., while you are out. These are generally available from hardware and other specialist stores. Some are fitted with sensors which react automatically to approaching darkness, movement or noise.

Electronic security systems comprise two parts, a detector and an alarm. There are a number of sensor detectors which can be installed in the home. Some require wiring to a monitor system, others are self-contained wireless units which have their own in-built audible alarms. These sensors can be activated in a number of ways, for example, by movement of the intruder or by impact, such as breaking glass; others are activated by body heat and so on. This type of detector can

be linked to a central monitor at a security firm or to 'local' noise-producing alarms or flashing lights. Alarms to detect fire or smoke can also be installed. Costs will vary considerably from relatively simple battery-operated alarms to the more sophisticated electronic devices; basic costs are added to when linked to full security systems and central monitoring firms. It needs to be remembered that alarms must be turned off and on before entering or leaving the home. This also applies to opening windows and doors while they are activated. Although alarm systems are being continually refined for simple operation, they may still cause difficulty for some people.

To find out what will work for you, and how to install such equipment, you can talk to the staff at a security firm or electronic goods store who will be happy to give more detailed information (there are always a number listed in the advertisement section of your telephone directory). Or simply talk to a handyman as many of these products are relatively easy to operate and install. The Police Department will also offer advice on security matters.

There is no need to be paranoid with home safety, but do take stock of your situation and don't take unnecessary chances or offer ridiculously easy opportunities for unwanted entry into your home. Consider one of the perennials which fall into this category – if you must hide a spare key, do not use the most *obvious* places such as under doormats, meter boxes, pot plants, etc.

HANDY HINTS

If you disturb a burglar don't try to tackle him alone. Leave the house and call the police. If you live in a high risk area it might be worthwhile following a New York trick of leaving some cash on a hall table as you go out. When you open the front door on return you can see if the money has gone, without the risk of perhaps finding yourself trapped inside with a desperate thief.

As well as locks for windows and doors, a shatter resistant film is now available to protect glass surfaces. This plastic film can be applied to existing internal window surfaces. When tested it has been extremely difficult to break. The glass remains attached to the film when broken, this adds to its deterrent qualities as police advise that an intruder will rarely attempt to smash glass a second or third time.

As louvre windows are easily removed from outside consider having them replaced or permanently fixed. Grilles and decorative bars designed for home use can be fitted to help prevent easy entry.

If key-operated locks are installed, don't leave keys in the lock. They are best kept nearby for any emergency, but not within easy reach of would-be rapists or burglars. Having broken the window the lock could then be simply undone!

When it comes to home safety you can help prevent windows being forced – from the old, well-used, and no-cost deterrents, such as a large nail in the window sash (so the window cannot be easily forced up), to a piece of wood in the sliding window channel to help prevent it being forced sideways.

There are many effective locking devices and alarms available for windows too, and a retailer of home safety devices such as hardware or department stores can advise on the latest innovations.

Situation Alone at home at night, there is a knock at the door. Without thinking you open the door only to find yourself flung back against the wall as a stranger forces his way in. What could you have done to help avoid this situation?

Defence Whether you live alone or not, there will always be occasions when husband, family or friends are absent. A viewer, safety chain or security screen door will allow you to decide when, or whether, to open the door further, so always check first and be wise *before*, rather than after the event. These common sense precautions apply whether living in the city or in a rural environment.

> **HANDY HINT**
>
> Always have good lighting over doorways. There are lights which automatically switch on when sound activated such as someone knocking at the door. Others respond to movement by switching on immediately, this can provide a home safety 'extra', as any potential prowler is highlighted in a pool of light.

Situation Whether living in a block of units where there are many people around, or in a country area where the nearest neighbour may be kilometres away, you can still feel isolated. An attacker, taking advantage of your situation has forced his way inside. You struggle, breaking free from his grasp. However, in your panic you don't know which way to run, and find yourself trapped in a corner. What could you have done to avoid this?

Defence Consider the possibility of someone breaking in, and look at the layout of your own home. Ask yourself these questions – do I know which doors have locks? which windows can be easily opened? where the phone or phone extension is located? If you break away from the attacker which is your best escape route? Who can you run to for help?

Having considered your own situation then you have some constructive ideas in mind rather than blind panic, you now have a good chance to use those options.

HANDY HINT

Have a trial run, literally, out of the door or window . . . turning into a neighbour's house . . . and so on.

Situation You are sound asleep in bed, a sudden noise causes you to stir. Before you have gathered your senses together you find yourself pushed roughly back onto the bed by an intruder as you try to sit up. What can you do to gain the initiative and get to your feet fast.

Defence While one does not usually keep a specific weapon next to the bed, be aware of what you *could* use if necessary. For example, a book, torch, biro, brush, bedside lamp – in fact *any* object which is likely to be within reach can be effectively used to strike out, or hit at, the attacker even rendering him unconscious if hit hard enough. Remember to improvise when necessary. People have been known to use many innovations of their own – from a knitting needle placed under the pillow to a hockey stick or baseball bat kept next to the bed!

Self-Defence When Walking

Too many people are attacked or molested because they are unaware, or haven't bothered to take basic safety precautions, so learn to minimise these risks and consider some of the following safety rules.

Try not to walk alone late at night, and don't take short cuts which may take you through empty streets, car parks, or other deserted areas. Where practicable walk or jog facing the traffic, close to the kerb and as far as possible from obvious 'lurking' spots such as doorways, hedges and overgrown shrubbery.

If you have a regular routine of travel to and from the train, bus, school, and so on, vary your route from time to time so that you don't make it easy for a would-be assailant to pick *his time and place.*

Whenever possible keep to lit roads, even if this means going a little out of your way and, as you approach your car or home, have your keys *in your hand.* You are then ready for a speedy entry with little opportunity for any waiting attacker and you have the additional bonus of an immediate weapon in the hand, for a quick distraction strike.

A study by two New York psychologists concluded pedestrians may signal to criminals that

they are easy targets by the way they walk. The survey which covered equal numbers of men and women of varying ages, required a group of convicted prison inmates to give a 'muggability' rating on them. It was felt the study confirmed that 'dreaminess' and awkwardness in body movements read as signals for criminals to move in.

Always walk briskly and purposefully, with an air of confidence. Muggers are opportunists looking for easy targets – so don't give them that opportunity. Always be aware of your surroundings.

If you feel you are being followed while walking, change direction. Cross the road, move off at a tangent, walking briskly. Be prepared to run into the nearest shop or house if necessary. Be prepared to use your voice. Sometimes it pays to trust your intuition, even if you do feel a little foolish. It is better to be alert to possible dangers than to be caught unawares.

HANDY HINTS

When walking, particularly at night, you can carry a torch for light and as a weapon if necessary.

There are battery-operated security devices which function as a torch but can also emit a most earpiercing noise when a button is pressed.

A whistle can also be used to attract attention. For easy access the whistle can be put on a watch or other wrist band.

Situation While walking along the street a car begins to follow. You increase your pace trying to ignore it, but the car's speed is also increased. Feeling very frightened, what can you do?

Defence By making a 180-degree turn and running back the way you came, you gain a head start. By the time the car has U-turned (or reversed) you have time to make a hasty exit. You are able to change direction much more quickly than the car – more than once if necessary!

Situation Having just finished the afternoon shift you are on your way home when suddenly you are grabbed savagely by the hair from behind and dragged backwards. What can you do?
Defence If grabbed by the hair then your first reaction should be to *press your hands down* on top of the attacker's. Hold his hand (and your hair!) *tightly against your head*. This stops the pain allowing you time for countermeasures.

At the same time you can duck your head down and pivot round toward him. Now, still keeping a tight grip on the hand, really *jerk* your head *up sharply* – this twists his wrist, and puts you in a better position to retaliate.

Situation Alighting from your usual bus you take the short cut home to the next street through a vacant allotment. It is not far and you have gone the same way many times. Although there are no lights nearby you don't give it much thought. An assailant suddenly emerges from behind some shrubs and knocks you to the ground before you realise what is happening. What can you do?
Defence Vary your routine, don't give a potential attacker the advantage of being able to preplan time and place. Although it may mean going a little further out of your way, keep to well-lit areas rather than take a short cut through vacant blocks.

However if you are knocked down draw your arms and legs in as quickly as possible to give you some protection. You can then use both the surprise element and the power from your bent arms or legs to hit and kick out more effectively.

HANDY HINT

When knocked or pushed to the ground always try and get to your feet as quickly as possible. However as you may hit the ground with some force and can't easily get up, then roll quickly onto your back and draw your legs and arms in (bring knees towards chest). By drawing your arms and legs in you are able to more effectively hit out, using both surprise and the striking force from a bent arm or leg. You don't have to be strong but aim your strike at more vulnerable points such as knee, groin and so on. Don't just 'bicycle' aimlessly, it's too easy for your legs to then be grabbed.

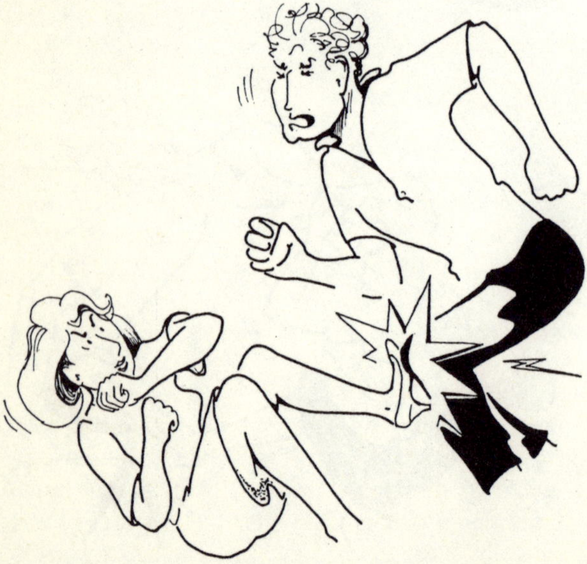

Car Safety

Prevention is the best self-defence and car safety falls very neatly into this category. Always make sure your car is locked before leaving, and on return check the back seat *before getting in.* If someone has forced an entry (or found an unlocked door!) you will not be taken by surprise from behind. However should this happen and you are grabbed, be prepared to quickly pull the keys from the ignition and stab them into the intruder. This could be a sharp blow into the offending hand or the keys could be raked down an arm or into the face. Sufficient pain should be inflicted to enable you to break free and get out of the car. Have a practice quickly taking the key out of the ignition so you know exactly what you can do.

Another common sense measure which may prevent unnecessary stranding in an unknown, and perhaps potentially dangerous location, is to make sure your car is kept in sound mechanical condition, and always keep coins for an emergency phone call in the car. How often do we find we don't have the correct change with us when we need it!

An extra safety precaution when travelling to a destination you are unfamiliar with, particularly at night, is to estimate the time you may take en route, including any places you will be stopping. You are then able to leave your proposed destination with someone, and an estimated time for your return.

Do not pick up hitch-hikers. Dependent on circumstances at the time, if someone signals they are in trouble you can drive to the nearest garage or police station to seek assistance on their behalf.

> **HANDY HINTS**
>
> Vary parking places as much as possible and always try and park in a well-lit area.
>
> Have your keys *in your hand* when entering a car park – don't make it easy for any would-be assailant.

Situation Driving home alone, you stop at an intersection. The passenger door is suddenly wrenched open and a stranger leaps in. What should you have done?

Defence If alone in a car always drive with doors locked and the passenger windows *up.* A simple rule but this may save you from a potentially dangerous situation.

Situation You are driving home alone at night but feel you are being followed by someone in the car behind. As it becomes obvious that you are indeed being followed and you know your home is empty, what can you do?

Defence Don't drive straight home, but rather drive to the nearest police station – it may be a little further out of your way, but if you are being followed then it is better to be safe than sorry. Another alternative is to drive into a service station or some other populated place rather than to an empty house. Preplanning can save a lot of worry.

Abusive Or Obscene Phone Calls

This type of call can be very distressing to anyone on the receiving end. A person who makes abusive or obscene phone calls preys on your unpreparedness, and having caught you off guard takes advantage of it. The best advice is to slam the phone down fast and *say nothing.* Telecom advise that many nuisance calls tend to be random, so don't give the caller the satisfaction of a reaction on your part – often that is the 'thrill' of the call. If there is no comment they don't know if they've reached their target. Certainly never say you are alone, and don't answer the phone giving your name, just 'hello' is preferable as it gives nothing away. You may ask what number *they* were calling before quoting your own number thus giving very little for an inquisitive caller to go on.

If the caller persists report details to the appropriate authority – such as Telecom, who have their own system for dealing with these calls. Additionally you can keep a whistle handy – one sharp blast should keep his ears ringing for days!

A recent newspaper report gave some interesting background on how the Japanese beat the heavy breathing brigade. With an average of almost 9000 reported calls a month, electronic experts in Japan are turning the life of the obscene caller into

a high tech nightmare with devices which assault both his ears and his sensibilities. To cool the ardour of the heavy breather there is a machine which repeats in a male voice 'hello, hello', 'who's there?' and 'the person you want isn't here for the moment'. A persistent caller gets hit with a deafening whistle. If that doesn't work there is perhaps the ultimate weapon – the sound of the caller's own voice. The makers of this device claim that telephone maniacs are put off if they hear themselves. Yet another model turns the tables by identifying the caller's own telephone number.

HANDY HINT

As already noted calls are often made at random, 'on spec' so don't advertise your telephone number, or personal details unnecessarily. For example, a common advertisement would be 'wanted . . . to share flat or house'. Consider carefully how much detail *is necessary* before adding your home phone number. Do you really need to list age group, name, marital status, etc? Think about it, just how many do?

You can avoid putting yourself in an awkward position by being alert to the possible danger beforehand.

For Young People

We all have the right to protect ourselves, regardless of age, so if you are six or sixteen you have *the right to say 'no'* if someone asks you to go with them. From an early age we are told not to go with strangers but strangers aren't always that easy to recognise. They can be men and women, come in all shapes and sizes, and be of any age. Of course not all strangers mean us harm. Many people quite genuinely like to be friendly and talk to young people, so again you can be friendly – you can be polite – but you can say 'no'.

No-one wants to live in a world where we don't talk to, or won't help each other, but always be alert and don't give anyone the opportunity to hurt you. Here are some simple rules to remember.

If questioned by a stranger, whether in person or on the phone, *don't* tell them you are alone. You can always pretend some adult person is also there, for example, Mum, Dad, brother – any name will do.

If you're home by yourself ask for identification before letting anyone in and that includes such 'essential' people as the TV repair man! Any trades person who has a genuine reason to call will have identification or won't mind if you want to ring up and check.

Sometimes people we know can mean us harm, too, so if you find yourself in this situation and aren't sure what you should do, then be prepared to tell a parent, teacher or another adult what happened, rather than worry if you did the right thing or not. Again remember you can say 'no'.

Another awkward and potentially frightening situation young people quite often find themselves in is when people play on their vulnerability to embarrass and frighten them, for example, by exposing themselves. People who do this are generally called 'flashers'. This is a word we often associate with comedy routines on television which usually have a man in a raincoat 'flashing' it open and – we all know he has no clothes on underneath! It can seem very funny on television, but not so funny if a real person does this to you. Usually people mean you no physical harm but it can be a nasty shock. Remember it's *not your fault* if this does happen, and you haven't done anything to cause this person to pick on you, it could in fact have happened to anyone who came along. So again, tell your parents or another adult if it happens. It's important, so the person concerned can't continue to frighten other young people or perhaps become more aggressive.

When you have to catch a bus or train, know your timetables so you don't find yourself standing around for a long time just waiting. Be aware of places where you are more likely to run into trouble such as deserted buildings, school grounds, car parks and so on.

If you miss your bus home or you're just plain late, keep the necessary coins with you to ring and let someone know where you are and check what you should do.

Don't hitch-hike or just wander off by yourself. Know where the nearest public phones are and how to use them. Have a plan worked out so you know what to do.

Remember some of the tricks people can use to try and get you to go with them. They may ask you to help them search for a lost pet or some money they have dropped – don't go wandering off behind hedges, bushes, sheds, etc. You may also find yourself offered a reward to go with them, but always say you must check with an adult person first.

If you are asked a question such as the name of a street or where someone lives, you can answer but always keep some distance between yourself and the questioner. This enables you to quickly run off should that be necessary.

If you find yourself being hassled while travelling on the train be prepared to get off at the next station and change carriages to one with more people. Also be wary of groups and strangers who tend to hang around places such as amusement parks, video/games parlours where they know young people are more likely to gather.

Avoid, whenever possible, using toilets in parks and other more remote areas. It is better to use toilets in department stores, libraries, museums, and other public buildings where there are likely to be regular staff on duty.

Another good idea is to think of the things you could use to help you get away if someone should try and grab you or take you away:

- you can kick, bite, yell
- you can run – flat out.

There are many things you are likely to have with you which can be used to gain a temporary advantage. A hefty school bag dropped on feet or swung at legs can help! In fact almost anything you are likely to have with you can be used as a distraction, such as biros or locker keys which can be used to

strike or jab at the assailant. Make a list, you may even surprise yourself with what you discover you can do.

Situation While walking home a stranger calls from a parked car and politely asks directions. You unconsciously step forward to answer but find yourself being bundled into the car. What should you have done?

Defence Don't step up to a car or person. Don't allow anyone the opportunity to grab you (if that is their intention). You can still be heard just as clearly keeping one or two paces' distance between you.

For Parents

People are now more conscious of the need to offer children every possible assistance and advice for their safety to protect them against assault, intimidation and molestation. While figures of the instance of these crimes have risen in recent years, there is a lot we can do to help ourselves, and at the same time help protect our children. It's important to note that not all assault, harassment and intimidation of children comes from strangers. One survey showed 77 per cent of the attackers were acquainted with or well known to the victim and in the same survey 51 per cent of all victims of rape, sexual assault and incest were 15 years or under. Victims in this age group were most often attacked by people in positions of authority and trust such as a relative, neighbour or babysitter. So be conscious of this, not paranoid, but be prepared to listen to what your children may have to say. Think ahead, sometimes self-defence can be simply using common sense precautions, so let's look at a few. You can check your own home safety arrangements both for when you are there, *and* when the children are by themselves or with a babysitter.

There are a few questions we need to ask ourselves. For example, do they know what to do or say if someone calls at the door or rings up while you are out? What should they do if approached on the street or leaving school? What should they do if they've missed the bus or other public transport? The answers are simple enough but we need to talk about the problems and be quite clear on the necessary response to make. These questions have already been discussed in other sections of the book, but briefly look at home security first and make sure it is not easy for someone to just walk into your home. Make sure the children know how, and do use, any safety devices you have and that they in fact don't open the door first and ask questions later!

Make sure they know that if approached by a stranger, whether that person is on foot or in a car, they *do not step up close* to answer any questions put to them and that they do not go with someone they are not sure of, regardless of the pretext used. You could try making up a few examples yourself of the type of tricks that are used and work out together how to avoid them.

When it comes to missed buses and so on ensure they carry the necessary coins to phone and that they do know where phone boxes are and how to use them. Also there is a need to stress that they should *not hitch-hike* but ring someone first, before ever thinking of attempting to set out by themselves.

There is a scheme called Safety House. Perhaps it is something you are already familiar with, or you may like to consider introducing it to your own neighbourhood. Details may be obtained through your Police Department. Safety House offers school children protection from potential molesters. Where this scheme has operated both within Australia and overseas lower child molestation rates have resulted. In simple terms a Safety House is one where a child can go if approached by a stranger. Someone in that designated (and approved) Safety House has agreed to be home from 8-9 a.m. and 3-4 p.m., and able to contact police and parents if necessary. It is a community involvement programme, everyone has very clear guidelines and instructions on how it works and what to do. Houses involved are clearly marked with a small plaque and children are well instructed in the operation of the scheme.

It is important to realise that this scheme only operates officially in school times and is not a guarantee that people are there at all other times. Therefore children should be made aware of all alternative personal safety procedures, in case they are necessary.

Situation You are alone at home, or at home with young children. The phone rings, the caller is unknown. It soon becomes clear this caller wants to know if you are alone. You hang up, but it leaves you feeling very insecure.

Defence Most important do not let the caller know you are alone, and don't answer his questions without first thinking of the consequences. If the call is harmless then you can remain polite but firm – give no information which could be used by a potential attacker or thief.

Make sure the children also understand this – explain why. They can be surprisingly quick to understand, and it is for their protection too.

> HANDY HINT
>
> Do not list your full name in the telephone directory – just initials is preferable.

For Babysitters

If you are babysitting many simple safety precautions for not only yourself, but the children you are taking care of, have already been discussed. However to reinforce these safety hints consider the following.

Know whom to call in an emergency and always have a phone number where the parents can be contacted – an extra 'back-up' number is also a good idea.

Don't let someone in without knowing who they are, you can check identification, even if it means a phone call. When answering the phone yourself don't alert the caller to the fact that you are alone.

It's a good idea to know the general layout of the house, which doors have locks and so on. If there is a viewer or safety chain on the door then be prepared to use them *before* letting someone in.

Knowing what you can do, should the need arise, means that you can settle down and enjoy your babysitting – that is if the children co-operate too!

Self-Defence For Elderly People

Too often older people, of either sex, are seen as easy targets for attack, robbery or harassment. The need for a knowledge of practical common sense self-defence hints applies equally to men and women. While in the past women may have been considered more at risk, assaults on elderly men have also increased.

Although many aspects of personal safety have been looked at already, let's check through some of those which apply directly to elderly people. Pre-plan your safety. This simply means don't wait until something does go wrong, for example, a burglary, handbag stolen, personal abuse and so on. Ask someone, such as a member of the family or a friend, to help work out what best suits your needs. Discuss your particular situation with them and consider what will work, and is practical *for you*, including possible costs.

Home security devices can range from the relatively inexpensive, under twenty dollars, through to hundreds and even thousands of dollars if very sophisticated electronic equipment is contemplated or warranted. Knowing what resources are available and what will work for you, gives a greater peace of mind, and may well be considered a worthwhile investment.

But first look at your own home. We all tend to be rather complacent until something happens to us. Make a list of possible danger areas, for instance do you have louvre windows which can easily be removed? Do you leave windows open for ventilation, particularly in the bedroom? If this is the case then consider some of the key-operated locks on the market which allow a window to be left partially open, yet still provide protection against easy entry.

There are many other security devices, varying from basic battery-operated alarms which can be easily fitted to windows and doors – a loud alarm is triggered when the fitting is opened – to wired systems such as with reed switches. These switches are connected to a control panel which then activates the alarm system.

Safety chains, door limiters and viewers allow the householder to see who the caller is *before* letting him in, and security doors are also excellent for this purpose. It is best to have solid external doors both *front and back*, with deadlocks and again security doors which make entry extremely difficult for a would-be burglar or assailant. Good lighting over doorways is another important safety factor when assessing callers, and always check who it is at the door *before* letting someone in. Always ask for identification. If you are not convinced, say you are going to telephone the company or the police to check. The caller won't mind if they're genuine, and if not they'll be off down the street before you've lifted the receiver. Remember the caller won't know if you've got a phone or not!

Consider other points of entry into your home and again decide what is most practical for you to use as a deterrent. This means not only thinking what will keep intruders out, but what will also allow you to leave quickly in an emergency.

Never let anyone know you are by yourself, either at the door or on the phone. You can always pretend there is someone else with you – son, nephew, husband, for instance. You can even call out as if to someone – any name will do, but preferably male. If someone asks for personal information on the phone, for example, they may say they are from a bank, or some other financial organisation and want details on your income, it is important to note *you do not have to give personal information to anyone.* If you feel the request warrants a response, ask them to put their enquiry in writing and in the mail.

For greater peace of mind and safety a phone next to the bed is a useful aid. By purchasing an extension cord and telephone double adaptor from Telecom an existing phone system can be used with little additional cost.

Good preplanning also includes having the police emergency number next to your telephone and also your local police station number. If you think there is a prowler or peeping tom around then you have the number to ring readily at hand.

You can prearrange a distress signal with a neighbour, for example, or you may feel it worth considering a personal alarm system for extra peace of mind. One or more security buttons, also called 'panic buttons', can be installed in a house so that an alarm can be triggered if a prowler is heard, or for some other emergency such as a medical one. Security buttons are usually installed in bedrooms and sometimes the kitchen or other strategic spots in the house. The alarm can have twenty-four-hour monitoring if connected to a central station (costs would include a monitoring fee), or it can be connected via a telephone link (auto-dialler) to a relative, friend or other nominated emergency number. The alarm can also be connected to an outside siren, bell or flashing light to alert neighbours or passers by.

It may be an idea to consider a pet, even a small dog can make enough noise to alert you if some-

one is about, and many dogs can be a deterrent in themselves. However it is not wise to rely too heavily on an animal for your total protection as a dog can bark at the wrong things (stray cats, for example), and sometimes not at all when it is needed! They should be considered as a definite plus factor, but in some areas particularly home units, rented accommodation and so on, pets are not allowed. You are your own best protector when you know *what you can do*.

Beware of con men who prey on those living alone, particularly the elderly, so think *before* answering questions and do not give personal details away. Confidence tricksters are usually very convincing, and can come in many guises. They may say they are conducting a census, collecting for a charity, have come to read the meter or to give a quote on any number of things from window cleaning to new carpet. The important point is not to let *anyone* in without checking their credentials first. Again if in doubt, check with the firm or organisation they claim to represent. If you have arranged for a representative or trades person whom you don't know to call, and you are a little worried then simply ask a friend over to be there at that time.

Now let's look at some safety factors when outside the home, so that we feel comfortable when travelling, on holidays or simply doing the weekly shopping. If you feel uneasy about walking by yourself, where possible arrange to walk with a companion or a group.

If you are on foot, be alert and walk purposefully. Whatever you're carrying – a shopping bag, walking stick, umbrella – be prepared to use it! Don't carry your purse on top of a shopping bag, making yourself an obvious target for any potential thief. Money should be kept out of sight.

In the street, if stopped and asked a question, however innocent it may seem, keep some distance between you and the questioner. A favourite mugger's trick is to approach someone walking alone. Women, particularly elderly, are most at

risk, but men have been attacked also. They may ask for direction, or the time, then, while your attention is diverted, grab your bag or purse.

At night walk on the lighted side of a street, avoiding doorways, darkened laneways, bushes and so on. And it's a good idea to carry a small torch with you because it can be used not only for its light but also as an emergency weapon!

Always have your keys out ready for smooth entry into your home or car and be prepared to use them as a distracting weapon to jab into an assailant, giving you the chance to get away and summon help. There are also personal alarms available which emit an ear-piercing noise to frighten away an attacker or even a dog. However it should be noted that like all mechanical devices

there is always the chance of malfunction, or it could be dropped in an emergency. So be prepared to use your voice too; you could have a whistle on a wrist band as an extra means of creating noise.

If you are driving, park in a well-lit area and drive with your doors locked and windows up. There are a number of other basic precautions you can take when driving which are covered further in the car safety section of this book. Read it too.

> **HANDY HINT**
>
> Modern phones provide for your most frequently called or emergency numbers to be stored in the phone's memory. This then enables a call to be made by simply pressing one or two buttons (depending on your phone type).

Situation Sick, elderly, disabled, unable to move quickly? An assailant forces his way into your home. What can you do?

Defence Attitude is most important, *you are not helpless.* Give some constructive thought to what *you can do* to help yourself in such a situation. Talk it over with a friend or relative. First consider your 'frontline' safety, that includes home security devices – be prepared to use them. Check identification before letting someone in.

If someone has forced their way inside, don't let yourself be panicked into a corner with nowhere to go – think which doors have locks and how you could get out in an emergency.

An equally important consideration is to prearrange, with say your neighbours, a signal which will alert them that you are in trouble. This allows help to be quickly summoned. Have a phone next to the bed and don't forget there are safety products such as security buttons and wireless intercoms which can be installed.

HANDY HINT

How you alert someone to your difficulties can vary – from the use of electronic equipment, to a low cost bell system to a neighbour who can also summon help when needed.